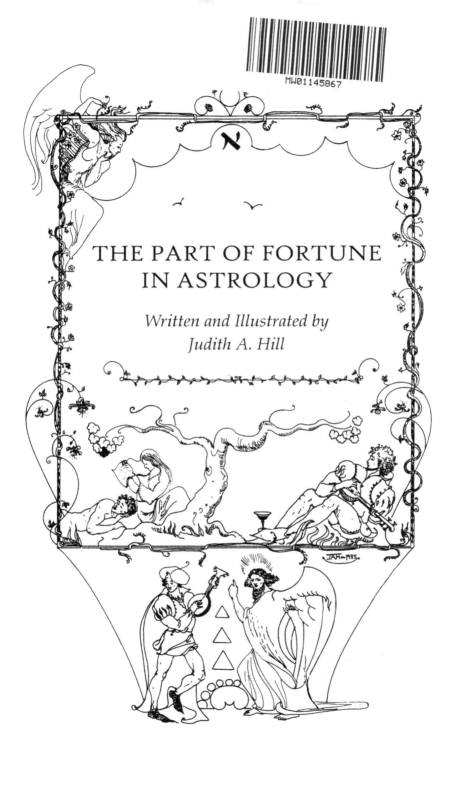

THE PART OF FORTUNE IN ASTROLOGY

Written and Illustrated by
Judith A. Hill

THE PART OF FORTUNE IN ASTROLOGY

cover and interior art by Judith Hill
cover design by Seth Miller

ISBN
1-883376-03-3 (1st edition)
978-1-883376-03-1 (2nd edition)

First edition 1998
Second edition 2010

STELLIUM PRESS

THE PART OF FORTUNE IN ASTROLOGY

CONTENTS

Chapter 1

What is the Part of Fortune?

A lone survivor of scores of "Arabic Parts" once commonly used, the *Part of Fortune* has solitarily remained a mainstay of western astrological practice. The recognition of this horoscopic "part" aka "lot" is very ancient and not at all of Arabic origin. Claudius Ptolemy discusses the Part of Fortune as one of five imminently important "hylegical," i.e. life-giving entities in his Tetrobiblios, 140 A.D.

Although the exact origin of the "parts" aka "lots" remains unclear, there is little doubt that Ptolemy copied much of his material from far earlier sources at the later-to-be-burned library of Alexandria. What seems certain is the high status that the Part of Fortune held in ancient astrology amongst the known as "parts," or "lots." Indeed, as one of five possible life span allotting points (including Sun, Moon, Ascendant degree and Midheaven degrees), the Part of Fortune must have been regarded as the verifiable queen of parts.

Perhaps there exists another reason for its popularity. As an exact projection of the solar-lunar phase relationship from the birth Ascendant degree, it was called the "place of happiness" by astrologers of a generation previous to ours, and indeed, will function as such. Oddly, this meaning seems lost among today's astrologers. We tend to value highly that which brings happiness.

Additional meanings attributed to the Part of Fortune, aka "Pars Fortuna," "Lot of Fortune", "Fortuna" or affectionately "Pars," will be dealt with presently.

The history and development of the "Arabic Parts" will not be included in this succinct work. This has already been accomplished for us in Robert Zoller's outstanding book entitled *The Arabic Parts in Astrology*.

The focus of this book is threefold: to introduce the Part of Fortune; to outline its three key meanings; and to provide interpretive suggestions for Pars Fortuna through the twelve astrological houses of the birth chart: the twelve zodiac signs; and also when found in conjunction with any of the eight known planets, the two lights (Sun and Moon), and the South and North Lunar Nodes.

Calculating the Pars Fortuna

Most computer programs include the Part of Fortune. However, you can easily calculate it for yourself by following these steps.

1) Add the zodiac sign *number* (**Aries is Sign 1, Taurus is 2, etc.**) of the Ascendant sign; and then the degrees and minutes for the Ascendant degree, *together* with that for the Moon. (See chart next page to find the zodiac sign number.)

Example: Let us pretend our Ascendant is at 20.35 degrees and minutes of Taurus (sign number 2) and our Moon is at 5.23 degrees and minutes of Aquarius (sign number 11).

This is how the addition of the two (Ascendant and Moon) should look: **(below, and also see example, Page 7.) Bold type is the zodiac sign number.**

Light type is the degree and minute.

2.20.35	Ascendant
11.05.23	Moon
13.25.58	The sum

2) **Subtract** from this sum, (13.25.58) the zodiac sign number, degrees and minutes of the Sun.

Let us pretend our Sun is at 10.40 degrees and minutes of Aries, the first sign.

13.25.58
1.10.40
12.15.18

Result: The 12th sign, Pisces, 15.18 degrees of this sign.

Note: If in your subtraction you "run out" of signs, simply add the number "12" (the whole round of signs) to your first sum (Ascendant and Moon), before subtracting the Sun's position. If your remainder exceeds 12, subtract 12.

The result is your old style "day birth" Pars Fortuna. It should mimic your true birth solar-lunar phase angle as projected in the natural order of signs from the Asc. degree.

SIGN NUMBERS FOR PARS CALCULATION

Aries **1**; Taurus **2**; Gemini **3**; Cancer **4**; Leo **5**; Virgo **6**;

Libra **7**; Scorpio **8**; Sagittarius **9**; Capricorn **10**; Aquarius **11**;

Pisces **12**.

Day Birth Pars / Night Birth Pars

Modern western astrologers use the day[1] birth Pars Fortuna for both day and night births. The ancient Greek and Arabic astrologers *reversed* the calculations for night births by projecting the solar-lunar phase relationship *backward* from the Ascendant.

Was this theoretical, or did it work? You will have to experiment with this yourself. I will be somewhat "heretical" by revealing my own experience, and that of many others: the "day birth" Pars, i.e., the *true natal solar-lunar phase projection from the Ascendant,* works very well for everyone, day and night birth alike. *At least it does so for the "three keys" of interpretation presented in this work.*

Possibly, this interpretive viability is one reason why western astrologers came to abandon the night birth calculation. However, this does not imply that the reversed natal solar-lunar phase as projected from the Ascendant, i.e., night birth Pars, has no important meaning, or that you should ignore it. Certainly it does. In fact, for day births, this point functions as the "Part of the Spirit," a sort of spiritual motivation point, somewhat poorly defined in old texts.

For night births, the true projection of the solar-lunar phase from the Ascendant (again, the "day birth" Pars), once traditionally functioned as the night birth Part of Spirit.

Every astrologer must do his or her own experimentation with pars and its alternative calculation for night births

[1] The Sun must be above the horizon line (Asc/Dec axis) for day births-below for night births.

From my own experience, and undoubtedly that of generations of western astrologers, the true projection of the natal solar-lunar phase from the Ascendant, *whatever you wish to call it*, works precisely as described in this book for day and night birth alike.

Is it possible that modern western astrologers haven't been "wrong," in that their single Pars method worked as needed, providing similar interpretive results for both day and night births? If it hadn't, wouldn't they have noticed it by now? Their apparent ignorance of the night birth reversed calculation did not effect the meaning of the true solar-lunar phase projection from the Ascendant for night births. However, what they missed out on is the meaning of a reversed projection of the solar-lunar phase from the Ascendant for *both* day and night births! And that is a subject for another booklet.

To reiterate: the **"day birth" Part of Fortune** is the **true projection** of the birth solar-lunar phase, projected by precise arc from the birth Ascendant degree in the natural order of the zodiac signs. *Alternative Definition:* the Part of Fortune is that zodiacal point in your natal chart that is equally distant from your Ascendant as the Moon is to your Sun in longitude.

The **"night birth" Part of Fortune** is the **reversed or inverted projection** of the solar-lunar phase, by precise arc projected from the birth Ascendant degree backwards, against the natural order of the zodiac signs.

Calculating the Night Birth Pars

If you wish to calculate the old "night birth" Pars Fortuna for night births, reverse the above formula (pages 2 -3) thus:

1) Add together the sign number (page 3), degrees and minutes of the Ascendant sign *together* with the sign number and degrees of the Sun.

2) From this sum, *subtract* the sign number, degrees and minutes of the Moon. **See example, page 8.**

Note: If the Moon's sign number is greater than the Sun's, therefore making it impossible to subtract, then add "12" to the combined sign number of Sun and Ascendant. Now you can subtract the Moon's sign number.

3) The remainder equals the zodiac sign degree and minute of the old style Part of Fortune for *night birth.*

Note: If you choose to calculate a night birth Pars in the ancient style, please do not neglect to also calculate the *true projection of the solar-lunar phase from the Ascendant* (as given on pages 2-3); and be sure to allot it the interpretive meanings given as Key 1 and 3 in this book (Chapter 2, page 9).

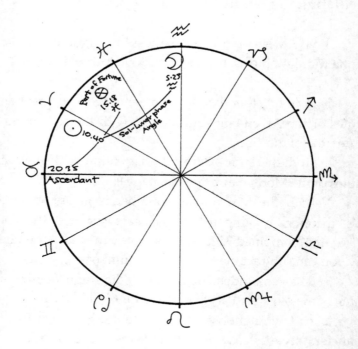

"DAY BIRTH" PART OF FORTUNE

Formula: Ascendant *plus* Moon, *minus* Sun.

This is the current "standard use" Part of Fortune for all
nativities, representing the true solar-lunar phase angle as
projected from the Ascendant degree in the natural order
of signs (counterclockwise: 1, 2, 3 etc.).
Ancient astrologers preferred this calculation for day birth
nativities.

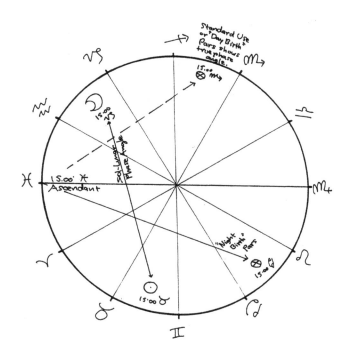

"NIGHT BIRTH" PART OF FORTUNE

Formula: Ascendant *plus* Sun, *minus* Moon (pg 6).

This is the currently neglected Part of Fortune position exclusively used for night birth nativities. However, it does *not* reflect the true solar-lunar phase angle as projected from the Ascendant (pages 2-3,7).

The Night Birth Pars placement *reverses* the true solar-lunar phase angle by being projected from the Ascendant degree in reverse of the natural order of the signs, i.e. clockwise from the Ascendant (e.g. 12, 11, 10...etc.)

8

Chapter 2

What the Pars Fortuna Means:
The Three Keys

Key 1: "The Place of Happiness"
Among the planets, there is no phase relationship more important than that of Sun and Moon. When the native's natal solar-lunar phase arc is projected from the natives' Ascendant, a point of harmony between the Sun, Moon and Ascendant is achieved fro that individual.

We are happy when we feel harmonious. Most people delight in the activities symbolized by the astrological house and sign position of their Part of Fortune. This is a joy spot, a little zone of bliss. Also, you will like whatever planet is closely conjunct Pars, having a taste for its affairs (Chapter 5, p 24).

Note: Delight, as an important, if not primary meaning of the Part of Fortune, has been essentially lost to astrologers of the present generation. Hopefully, this little work will return this meaning to circulation.

Key 2: Money
As the "Part of Fortune," this point is traditionally thought to suggest how and where you make your money. Also, you may profit from the activities symbolized by the house and sign position of Pars. Alternatively, you will profit from the house and sign placement of Pars' *dispositor*, i.e., the planet ruling the sign that your Pars is located in. Be sure to

include your "old style" sign rulerships, as given for each sign in Chapter 4, page 19.

If anything, the Part of Fortune is usually a bit lucky. People who are described by a planet your Pars conjoins will be generous to you, and various serendipitous events may occur in relation to any planet conjoined Pars, in combination with the house activities and zodiac sign character.

Pars should be used as an extra testimony of earnings, adjunct to the 2nd house and its rulers, as well as other important vocational planets. Indeed, financial success is indicated by the entire tone of a birth chart. A well placed Part of Fortune is an excellent *additional* testimony of financial success, but will rarely "cause" it on its own, unassisted by other factors in the birth chart.

(My book *Vocational Astrology* provides extensive detail on astrological vocational rulerships, and finances.)

A very strong wealth and success combination would consist of one of your natal vocational significators, i.e., planet rulers of the 10th, 6th, and 2nd houses, and especially the MC, to be simultaneously closely positioned conjunct both the natal Part of Fortune and the natal North Node!

Key 3: Correction

Pars Fortuna will either correct or improve a difficult or poorly placed natal planet. This is especially true in the case of the natal South Node, in that a conjunction of the South Node with Pars will negotiate some of the detrimental tendencies of the South Node. First, we must understand the four possible conditions of strength for any planet:

A) Very weak, "positive"
B) Very weak, "negative"
C) Very strong, "positive"
D) Very strong, "negative"

A) Pars Fortuna will decisively help with category **A** above: the very weak, positive planet. The term "positive" here means the suggested intention of this planet to act in a constructive manner. A conjunction of Pars will absolutely strengthen the function of a planet so debilitated. This planet will not turn out as poorly as otherwise suggested, and in fact, may indicate a real talent.

B) Pars will also strengthen a weak planet with "negative" intention. In some cases this is very fine. In other cases, this is like strengthening a bad habit. The planet is weak and negative, and the native delights in this! This is like going to hell, singing all the way.

C) Should Pars conjoin a very strong and positive planet, the results can seem miraculous. There seems to be nothing the native cannot accomplish along the lines of this strong planet. Great confidence and ability attend the traits associated with this planet in the natal chart. Additionally, the activities carried forth will be a positive nature, helpful; or at least not harmful. Still, the planet may suffer from too much of its own energy!

D) When Pars conjoins a strong planet with "negative" intention, we have a threatening situation.

This planet is given added force, and the luck to carry through its potentially negative activities. This can be likened to giving a tyrant carte blanche. One could revel unobstructed in his/her evil works and/or self-destruction.

Weak/Strong/Positive/Negative

Unfortunately, there is not space to discuss the conditions that betoken *weak, strong, negative,* and *positive.* This is an advanced technique and it is assumed that the astrological student possesses access to information assisting him/her in such determinations. If not, the student is guided towards getting a firm hand on the traditional "dignities" and "debilities" of the planets according to their natal house and sign placement. Old and outdated texts provide excellent starting material in this regard.

A mastery of the weak/strong/positive/negative determinations for natal planets is essential in any advanced branch of the astrological work.

Pars and the South Node

More is given on Pars/South Node on page 29.

Typically, a planet closely conjunct the South Node is weakened. This planet must "pay a karmic debt" in any number of interesting ways. We give out of this planet's energy, seldom receiving much in return. We must let of attachments to people or activities suggested by this planet.

However, should the Part of Fortune *also* be closely conjunct the planet/South Node duo, we foresee a correction entering the picture. The difficult issues indicated by the planet/

South Node conjunction will not be "all that bad." In some cases there appears to be no problem at all, as if Pars intervenes completely in correcting the promised weakness. In other cases the planet/South Node conjunction becomes a place of happiness rather than woe, and suggests the active exercise of rare talents gleaned from past lives; love of the past; and the enjoyment of spirituality.

Chapter 3

Pars Fortuna in the Twelve Houses

The suggestions below are general and for correct interpretation must be further refined by the consideration of the zodiac sign placement of the Pars Fortuna.

For example, Pars Fortuna in the 7th house enjoys associating with others. However, the zodiac sign will tell us how.

E.g. Pisces might suggest psychology; Virgo service; Libra marriage; Taurus financial physical, etc.

You must apply the quality and temperament of the zodiac signs to all house positions as listed below.

Keep in mind that each house "rules," i.e., bears an affinity with many more items than could possibly be listed here. In obtaining a more complete view of house rulerships, a copy of Rex E. Bill's *The Rulership Book* makes a useful companion.

P.F./1st House:

You like yourself and enjoy your own company. One testimony of a pleasant or striking appearance. People like your positive energy. Adds self-confidence.

Enhances earning power through the sign Pars occupies.

P.F./2nd House:

You enjoy money and fine things. Enjoyment is sought in food, ownership of material objects and body products.

Enhances earning power through the activities of the sign Pars occupies, and the placement of its dispositor.

P.F./3rd House:

Communication is your delight. You may like books, writing, talking, short journey, novelty or the fine arts. A younger sibling may bring joy. Fondness for siblings. Love of new experience.

Continued Enhances earning power through the activities of the sign Pars occupies, and that of its dispositor..

P.F./4th House:

Home and garden are special loves. You like your mother, nest, family, genealogy, the past, your past.

Earnings may relate to property, home, estate or family. Enhances earning power through the sign of Par's dispositor.

P.F./5th House:

You delight in pleasure, dance, romance and creative activities. Enjoyment is sought in art, sport, theatre, children and games. Your children, (at least your first child), bring joy.

Earnings may relate to recreational, artistic, sportive, creative, speculative activities. Enhances earning power through the sign placement of Par's dispositor.

P.F./6th House:

You like your work and get along with coworkers. Health, body or home improvement, and healing may be hobbies.

Earnings may relate to 6th house activities (above).

Corrects or reduces the potential of employment and health problems as may be shown in the natal chart.

P.F./7th House:

You love partnership and marriage and really like your partner. Consulting and counseling are enjoyable.

Earnings may relate to counseling, consulting, law, marriage, your partner or negotiations.

Assists or lightens effects of litigation and lawsuits.

P.F./8th House:

Sex, death and transformation are interesting to you.

Earnings may relate to psychology, healing, surgery, inheritance, insurance claims, investments, alimony or other people's money.

Corrects or reduces the impact of potential crises and/or chronic ailments.

P.F./9th House:

You love travel, education and/or religion, knowledge, and all things international.

Earnings may relate to academic pursuits, travel, ministry, teaching, publishing, places of knowledge, media, law, or advertising.

P.S./10th House:

Improves upon other career potentials shown in the chart. Your career is enjoyable and lucky. You may be fond of your father, landlord or boss. (Alternatively, you like to be one!)

P.F./11th House:

You love ideas, leisure and social events. Causal friends and group association are a real pleasure. Contributing to world good is a joy. Mental creativity comes easily.

Earnings may relate to idealized products, works of the imagination, collective works, groups, other people's children, companies, non profits or philanthropic activities.

P.F./12th House:

You love solitude, peace and spiritual work. Sleeping and sex are great pleasures. History, psychology, music and / or mysticism may be hobbies.

Earnings may relate to psychic work, hospitals, research, retreats and strange luck.

Corrects or reduces the impact of potential mental troubles, sufferings, and/or limitations of a karmic origin as shown in the birth chart. However, you may enjoy the very things that undo you because the 12th house is the proverbial "house of self-undoing".

Let There Be ~ ~Light

Chapter 4

Pars Fortuna in the Twelve Zodiac Signs

It is impossible to briefly summarize the full meaning of each sign, nor list all their manifestations. Therefore, the listings below rely on keywords to trigger further ideas in each astrologer's mind.

At the end of each entry is stated: "Earnings may relate to the activities of this sign as working out through the natal house position." *Activities* is a word selected to indicate the more visible applications of the sign's special energy. However, each sign "rules" or bears an affinity to several distinct occupations; and space limitations allow only a few of the more important listings.

A great deal of additional vocational and temperamental information about the twelve zodiac signs can be obtained from three suggested sources: *Vocational Astrology* and *The Astrological Body Types: Face, Form and Expression* by Hill; and Rex Bill's *The Rulership Book,* (See Bibliography).

P.F./Aries:

You love action, energy, discovery, adventure and spontaneous expression.

Earnings may relate to these Aries type activities as working through Pars' natal house position; and also to the natal house/sign placement of the planet *Mars*.

19

P.F./Taurus:

You love beauty, food, eating, forms, the senses, nature.

Earnings may relate to these Taurus type activities as working through Pars' natal house position; and also the natal house/sign placement of the planet *Venus*.

P.F./Gemini:

You love talking, communication, new experiences, mind stimulation, fun, humor, mental toys, play, coordinative games and talent development.

Earnings may relate to these Gemini type activities working out through the natal house position of Pars; and also the natal house/sign location of the planet *Mercury*.

P.F./Cancer:

You love home, nesting, family, mother, old memories, tradition, the past, ethnic and folk arts, music, tenderness, domesticity, emotional processing, food, nurturing, collections, sentimental feeling.

Earnings may relate to these Cancer type activities as working out through Pars' natal house position; and also the natal house/sign placement of the *Moon*.

P.F./Leo:

You love fun, drama, power, business development, the theater, youth, games, pleasure, art, sport, dance, your children, attention, creativity.

Earnings may relate to these Leo type activities as working out through the natal house position of Pars; and also the natal house/sign location of the *Sun*.

P.F./Virgo:

You love service, health, nutrition, body maintenance, work, animals, skills, data.

Earnings may relate to these Virgo type activities as working out through Pars' natal house position; and also the natal house/sign location of the planet *Mercury*.

P.F./Libra:

You love partnering, discussion and one-on-one focus, harmony, taste, balance, diplomacy, elegance, sweets.

Earnings may relate to these Libra type activities as working out through Pars' natal house position; and also the natal house/sign placement of the planet *Venus*.

P.F./Scorpio:

You love intensity, intimacy, concentrated emotion, manipulation of resources, death, sex, knowledge and power over the physical and psychological planes, transformation, healing, recycling, fragrance (smell), blending energies, the use of personal power.

Earnings may relate to these Scorpio type activities as working out through the natal house position of Pars; and also the natal house/sign placement of the planets *Mars* and *Pluto*.

P.F./Sagittarius:

You love travel of the mind or body! Teaching and learning are a joy. Delight is found in consciousness expanding activities, adventure, speed, risk and excitement.

Earnings may relate to Sagittarius type activities (above) as working out through the natal house position of Pars; and also the natal house/sign location of the planet *Jupiter.*

P.F./Capricorn:

You love achievement, mastery, authority, discipline, ownership, building, organizing, empire and self-perfection.

Earnings may relate to these Capricorn type activities as working out through Pars' natal house position; and also the natal house/sign placement of the planet *Saturn.*

P.F./Aquarius:

You love ideas, the imagination, philanthropy, experimental art or music, humor, new science, leisure, anthropology, people, the futuristic, individuality, rebellion, diversity, social activism, radical behavior, invention.

Earnings may relate to these Aquarius type activities working through Pars' natal house position; and also the house/sign location of the planets *Saturn* and *Uranus.*

P.F./Pisces:

You delight in solitude, rest, escape, whimsy, music, the imagination, romance, poetry, sex, emotional and psychic impressions, the past, the ocean, mysticism, compassion, charity, retreats.

Earnings may relate to these Pisces type activities as working through the natal house position; and also the natal house/sign of the planets *Jupiter* and *Neptune*.

Note: It was the opinion of renowned horary astrologer Ivy M. Goldstein, from her own experience, that a Piscean Part of Fortune functions as a "Part of Misfortune" in horary charts. It is unknown as to whether the same application can be claimed for natal charts.

Chapter 5

Pars Fortuna Conjunct Natal Planets, Sun, Moon and the North/South Lunar Nodes

P.F./Sun:

Happy disposition. Good self-esteem. Enjoys power. A good testimony of harmony with the husband. Strong vitality. One testimony of a long life.

Earnings may relate to some of the products, people or activities ruled by the Sun in combination with his house/sign placement: gold, husband, theater, management. Lucky. Strengthens a weak Sun. Improves a strong Sun.

P.F./Moon:

Fond of women, mother. A good testimony of harmony with the wife. Enjoys nurturing activities, especially if the Moon is in water and earth signs. Enjoys emotional expression through performance, (especially if the Moon tenants fire and air signs.)

Earnings may relate to some of the products, people or activities associated with the Moon in combination with her house/sign placement: silver, women, wife, public, music, acting, cooking, brewing, novels.

Luck with the public, women. Loves to travel.

A happy emotional life, should the Moon be otherwise free of ill aspects. May lengthen the life.

A debilitated Moon will be much improved if she is closely conjunct Pars Fortuna!

P.F./Mercury:

Loves books, writings, talking, mental stimulation and communication.

Earnings may relate to some of the products, people and activities associated with Mercury in combination with its house/sign placement: books, trade, writing, speaking, editing, accounting, technical and secretarial work, health, telephones, computers, communication equipment.

This conjunction much improves a debilitated Mercury. Enhances a strongly placed Mercury, promising talent!

P.F./Venus:

Loves beauty, pretty women, art, luxury, sweets, harmony, elegance, socializing, pleasure, romance, music.

Earnings may relate to some of the products, people and activities ruled by Venus in combination with her house/sign position: jewelry, fine clothes, hair and skin products, perfume, diamonds, girls, unmarried or young women, sweethearts, pleasure, gourmet food, music, art, wine, song.

Luck with love, gifts, women.

Improves a weak or debilitated Venus. Enhances a strong or dignified Venus.

P.F./Mars:

Loves action, energy, young men, competition, sport, war, law, healing, sharp tools, weaponry, fitness, making money.

Earnings may relate to some of the products, activities and people associated with Mars in combination with his natal

Note: If negative: too great a love for drugs, alcohol, fantasy, the underworld or night life, promiscuity. The native enjoys his/her addictions and dependencies.

Earnings may relate to some of the products, people and activities associated with Neptune in combination with his natal house/sign placement: i.e. photography, alcohol, oil, incense, devotional supplies, music, compassion, oceans, fish, glamor, videos, mysticism, psychic work, psychics, imagination, children's books, images, fads, the popular, poetry.

Lucky prayers and intuitions.

May correct or improve specific "leakage" problems associated with Neptune's placement in the natal chart. However, this placement can equally suggest that the native loves his/her additions.

P.F./Pluto:

Enjoys power, psychic intensity or emotional extremes. You may possess a strong will and/or supernatural talent i.e. thought manifestation, hypnotic ability, or unusual strength. Excellent for politicians and dramatists.

Earnings may be associated with some of the products, people and activities associated with Pluto in combination with his natal house/sign placement: excavations, refrigeration, the ancient past, immense wealth, destruction of the earth, tyrants, criminal activity (only if negative), research, surgery, insurance, nuclear industry, nuclear medicine, epidemics, ecological regeneration, extermination, death, chemicals.. This is one testimony of immense wealth if supported by additional factors in the horoscope.

Luck with power, research, transformation.

Corrects problems associated with a weak Pluto in the natal chart. Assist a strong Pluto, for good or ill.

P.F./North Node (Rahu, Dragon's Head, Caput):

A very successful and fortunate combination for the house/sign that Pars is located in at birth! The native enjoys success, power and material connections as related to the natal house/sign combination. Confidence is enhanced.

Earnings and general luck will absolutely be associated with the house/sign placement of this conjunction. Doubly fortunate for any planet simultaneously conjunct to both the North Node and the Part of Fortune!

Note: As much worldly opportunity is given, the native should take care not to become materialistic, selfish, egotistical or insensitive. The native is cautioned not to use the activities of this successful house/sign placement (and especially any planet conjoined) exclusively for self-aggrandizement, neglecting the greater concern for others.

P.F./South Node (Ketu, Dragon's Tail, Cauda):

The puzzle here is: Does Pars Fortuna correct the negative tendencies of the South Node? Or does the South Node ruin Pars? It seems to be a bit of both.

If *positive:* you may enjoy the past, history, mysticism; and you are well suited to spiritual life. You delight in the sweet and the good, and are generous, highly sensitive and non-materialistic.

You can easily access talents developed in past incarnations, and may show considerable natural genius in one or more fields. You may love spirituality, quiet and solitude (especially if Pars is found in water signs).

Note: If a planet is simultaneously conjunct the South Node and Pars, see pages 12-13.

If *negative:* you may delight in that which undoes you; enjoying addictions and those things that are not to your best interest. Also, you may loose what you love. Although you may well know what your bliss is, it may be extremely hard to find the time or support to follow this happy path. However, if you have this position and share these experiences, then look deeper! Vedic tradition specifies that Ketu teaches us the essential spiritual lesson of detachment.

A strong trine, sextile, conjunction or opposition from natal Jupiter; and/or a few strong and positive planetary combinations in your natal chart will partially or even completely antidote the negative potential of a natal Pars/South Node conjunction. The Moon's exact trine is especially helpful as is a close soft aspect from Pars' *dispositor,* i.e., planet ruler of the sign that Pars is located in.

Summary

Most birth charts are calculated with the inclusion of the Part of Fortune, yet so few of our generation know exactly how to interpret it! Hopefully, this succinct work will remedy this peculiar situation and return this important Part (aka "Lot") to interpretive circulation. There is no good reason why a horoscopic point once so essential to birth chart interpretation should remain in its present state of obscurity.

When interpreting Pars Fortuna, always remember the "Three Keys": *Happiness, Money,* and *Correction.*

Unfortunately, space does not allow the inclusion of working examples. Your own chart files should provide an abundance of test subjects.

Key 1: Happiness, or "a place of delight," will prove extremely accurate in the vast majority of cases. You may consider this the essential key to the Part of Fortune's interpretation. (This, however, is my personal opinion, as very ancient tradition emphasized Key 2.)

Key 2: Money, is a useful interpretation in only a certain percentage of cases; although an analysis of Pars' dispositor's house and sign placement will prove a fairly reliable descriptor of "from where the money comes."

Key 3: Correction, is useful only when Pars conjoins a planet in *need* of correction. We must use our commonsense in the wielding of this third important key.

*Here ends this little work on the interpretive
meaning of the Part of Fortune.*

BIBLIOGRAPHY

Robert Zoller, *The Arabic Parts of Astrology*, Inner Traditions international, Rochester, VT., 1980.

Claudius Ptolemy, *The Tetrobiblios*, 140 A.D., reprinted by The Aries Press, Chicago, 1936.

Andrea L. Gehrz (translator) *"An Introduction to the Tetrabiblios of Ptolemy, Porphyry of Tyre"*, Moira Press, 2010

Ivy M. Goldstein-Jacobson, *Simplified Horary Astrology*, (pages 17, 97, 116), Frank Severy Publishing, Alhambra, CA., 1960.

Geraldine Davis, *Horary Astrolgoy*, (page 21), First Temple of Astrology, Los Angeles, CA., 1970 (first printed 1942, by Symbols and Signs).

Rex E. Bills, *The Rulership Book*, Rex E. Bills, Richmond Virginia, 1976 (third printing).

Robert Hand and Robert Schmidt, "The Greek Track, " Tape Series, Project Hind Sight.

BOOKS BY THE AUTHOR

The Astrological Body Types, revised and expanded), Stellium Press, 1997 (available through Book People, A.F. A. Inc.)
Note: Russian and Lettish language editions available through Astroinformservis, Latvia.

The Part of Fortune in Astrology, Stellium Press, 1998, 2010

Vocational Astrology: A Complete Handbook of Western Astrological Career Selection and Guidance Techniques, A.F. A. Inc., 1999

The Mars-Redhead Files, Stellium Press, 2000 (compendium of published astro-genetic research by Hill and Hill-Thompason)

Astroseismology: Earthquakes and Astrology, Stellium Press, 2000 (compendium of published research by Hill and Hill-Polit))

Medical Astrology: A Guide to Planetary Pathology, Stellium Press, 2005

Mrs. Winkler's Cure: Stellium Press, 2010 (original fairy tales published under pen name Julia Holly).

The Lunar Nodes: Your Key to Excellent Chart Interpretation, Stellium Press, 2010.

JOURNAL ARTICLES BY THE AUTHOR

"The Mars–Redhead Link", Judith A. Hill & Jacalyn Thompson, *NCGR Journal,* Winter 88-89 (first published by *Above & Below* (Canada); *Linguace Astrale* (Italy); *AA Journal* (Great Britain); *FAA Journal* (Australia)

"The Mars Redhead Link II: Mars Distribution Patterns in Redhead Populations", *Borderlands Research Sciences Foundation Journal,* Vol. L1, No 1 (Part 1) and Vol. L1, No 2 (Part 2) "Commentary on the John Addey Redhead Data", *NCGR Journal,* Winter 88-89 "Redheads and Mars", *The Mountain Astrologer,* May 1996

"Correlation of Earthquakes with Planetary Placement: The Regional Factor", Judith A. Hill & Mark Polit *NCGR Journal*, 5 (1), 1987

"The Regional Factor in Planetary-Seismic Correlation", *Borderlands Research Sciences Foundation Journal*, Vol. L1, Number 3, 1995 (reprint courtesy of American Astrology)

"American Redhead's Project Replication", *Correlation*, Volume 13, No 2, Winter 94-95

"Octaves of Time", *Borderlands Research Journal*, Vol. L1, Number 4, Fourth Quarter, 1995

"Gemstones, Antidotes for Planetary Weaknesses", *ISIS Journal*, 1994

"Medical Astrology", *Borderlands Research Journal*, Vol. L11, Number 1, First Quarter, 1996

"Astrological Heredity", *Borderlands Research Journal*, 1996

"The Electional and Horary Branches", *Sufism, IAS*, Vol. 1, No 2

"Astrology: A Philosophy of Time and Space", *Sufism, IAS*, Vol. 1, No 1

"Natal Astrology", *Sufism, IAS*, Vol. 1, No 3

"An Overview of Medical Astrology", *Sufism, IAS*, Vol. 1, No 4

"Predictive Astrology in Theory and Practice", *Sufism, IAS*, Vol. 11, No 1

"Esoteric Astrology", *Sufism, IAS*, Vol. 11, No 2, 3

"Mundane Astrology", *Sufism, IAS*, Vol. 11, No 4

"Vocational Astrology", *Sufism, IAS,* Parts 1 and 2, Vol. 111, No 1, 2

"Astro- Psychology", *Sufism, IAS,* Vol. 111, No 3, 4

"The Planetary Time Clocks", *Sufism, IAS,* Vol. 4, No 1, 2, 3, 4

"Astrophysiognomy", *Sufism, IAS,* Vol. 4, No 1, 2

"Spiritual Signposts in the Birth Map", *Sufism, IAS,* Vol. V, No 2, 3

"The Philosophical Questions Most Frequently Asked of the Astrologer", *Sufism, IAS,* Vol. 5, No 4, Vol. 6, No 1, 2

"Music and the Ear of the Beholder", *Sufism, IAS,* 1999

"The Astrology of Diabetes", *Dell Horoscope,* October 2003

"A Life Time of Astrology", published interview with the author by Tony Howard, *The Mountain Astrologer Magazine, Nov-Dec, 2010*

Printed in the USA
CPSIA information can be obtained
at www.ICGtesting.com
CBHW070811180924
14359CB00049B/1098

9 781883 376031